JAMES ELAZZI is an award-winning playwright, screenwriter, and director renowned for amplifying marginalised and unheard voices. His compelling work has earned nominations at the NSW Premier's Literary Awards for three consecutive years, culminating in his 2024 win of the Martin-Lysicrates Prize. He has also been shortlisted twice for the Rodney Seaborne Award, received three nominations for the Sydney Theatre Awards, and is a three-time Silver Gull Playwriting Award nominee.

In 2024, James served as Assistant Director on *Holding the Man* at Belvoir St Theatre. He has made significant strides in film, writing, directing, and producing his second short film, *Seeds of Gold*, which explores Lebanese migration. This film has garnered the 2024 Panavision Award from the Australian Lebanese Film Festival and has been officially selected for eight international film festivals, including those in France, Florence, Prague, Lebanon, and Sydney.

James' first short film, *Yannis*, directed and produced in 2022, achieved remarkable recognition, being selected for over 17 film festivals worldwide, including events in Los Angeles, Poland, Lebanon, Greece, and Italy. It won Best Performances at the 2022 LGBTQI+ Los Angeles Film Festival and garnered seven nominations at the Made in The West Film Festival, winning Best Lead Actor.

His sold-out stage plays include *Saints of Damour* (2024 Qtopia Sydney), *Karim* (2024, National Theatre of Parramatta), *Son of Byblos* (Belvoir St Theatre 25A), *Lady Tabouli* (National Theatre of Parramatta), *Queen Fatima* (National Theatre of Parramatta), and *Omar and Dawn* (KXT). Through his dynamic storytelling, James continues to challenge narratives and inspire change in the arts.

Youssef Sabet as Karim and Andrew Cutcliffe as Joe in The National Theatre of Parramatta's production of K<small>ARIM</small> 2024. (Photo: Phil Erbacher)

KARIM
James Elazzi

CURRENCY PRESS
The performing arts publisher

CURRENCY PLAYS

First published in 2025
by Currency Press Pty Ltd,
Gadigal Land, Suite 310, 46–56 Kippax Street, Surry Hills, NSW 2010, Australia
enquiries@currency.com.au
www.currency.com.au

Copyright: *Introduction: Between Worlds* © Joanne Kee, 2025; *Karim* © James Elazzi, 2025.

COPYING FOR EDUCATIONAL PURPOSES

The Australian *Copyright Act 1968* [Act] allows a maximum of one chapter or 10% of this book, whichever is the greater, to be copied by any educational institution for its educational purposes provided that that educational institution [or the body that administers it] has given a remuneration notice to Copyright Agency [CA] under the Act.

For details of the CA licence for educational institutions contact CA, 12 / 66 Goulburn Street, Sydney, NSW, 2000; tel: within Australia 1800 066 844 toll free; outside Australia 61 2 9394 7600; fax: 61 2 9394 7601; email: memberservices@copyright.com.au

COPYING FOR OTHER PURPOSES

Except as permitted under the Act, for example a fair dealing for the purposes of study, research, criticism or review, no part of this book may be reproduced, stored in a retrieval system, or transmitted in any form or by any means without prior written permission. All enquiries should be made to the publisher at the address above.

No part of this book may be used or reproduced in any manner for the purpose of training artificial intelligence technologies or systems without the express written permission of the author and the publisher.

Any performance or public reading of *Karim* is forbidden unless a licence has been received from the author or the author's agent. The purchase of this book in no way gives the purchaser the right to perform the play in public, whether by means of a staged production or a reading. All applications for public performance should be addressed to the author c /— Lisa Mann Creative Management; PO Box 3145, Redfern NSW 2016; +61 2 9387 8207; info@lmcm.com.au.

Typeset by Brighton Gray for Currency Press.
Cover image shows Youssef Sabet; photo by Kathy Luu; image design by Hours After for Riverside's National Theatre of Parramatta. Cover design by Mathias Johansson for Currency Press.

Currency Press acknowledges the Traditional Owners of the Country on which we live and work. We pay our respects to all Aboriginal and Torres Strait Islander Elders, past and present.

Contents

Introduction: Between Worlds *Joanne Kee*	*vii*
Writer's Note	*xiii*
Karim	1

Youssef Sabet as Karim in The National Theatre of Parramatta's production of KARIM 2024. (Photo: Phil Erbacher)

Introduction: *Between Worlds*

James Elazzi grew up on a fifteen-acre farm in Tahmoor, New South Wales—a small rural town nestled on the edge of Western Sydney. His parents, Lebanese immigrants, worked the land growing cucumbers and tomatoes destined for Flemington Markets. Theirs was a life of labour, of early mornings and calloused hands, of seasonal rhythms and unpredictable yields.

For James, childhood unfolded between the rustling of greenhouse plastic and the stillness of the surrounding bush. His companions were not classmates or neighbourhood kids, but rocks, trees, animals and the vastness of the natural world. His imagination became his escape, his source of play, and ultimately his portal into storytelling. It is in this deeply personal landscape that *Karim* finds its roots.

This is not a nostalgic tale, however. This is a work of emotional clarity and cultural complexity that dares to speak diasporic truths that have long been left unsaid on Australian stages. It is a play about family, identity, ambition and love. It is about growing up between worlds, between cultures, expectations and desires. It is about being seen and the aching weight of not being seen.

The Tahmoor of James' past—where *Karim* is set—was isolated, primarily rural and shaped by the slow pace and hard realities of farming life. When James lived there, the town had a simple row of shops—including a takeaway called Skippy's, a train station and the natural wonder of Mermaid Pools.

One day, a neighbour had a stroke and died while waiting for an ambulance. This was the catalyst for James' family deciding to leave their property. That sense of isolation, of being cut off—not just geographically, but emotionally and systemically—echoes throughout the play.

Karim shines a light on those living on the margins: parents whose poverty feels insurmountable, who survive from day to day, who place the weight of their dreams, desires and fear of loneliness onto their children. James has created a portrait not just of a town, but of an emotional ecosystem that is imbued with the tension of generational expectation—the love that parents feel for their children and the sacrifices they demand in return. It explores the cost of ambition.

In the play, the tension lives in the central character's struggle: Karim wants more. More opportunity, more space, more possibility. But his father wants to keep him close. The result is a betrayal, a reshaping of history that binds Karim to a life not of his choosing. It's a story painfully familiar to many children of migrants: the guilt of wanting more than your parents had, and the grief of knowing your freedom might come at the cost of their dreams.

What makes *Karim* so striking is the way it weaves these big questions through the texture of everyday life. The play doesn't unfold in grand monologues or operatic confrontations—rather, it pulses through subtle gestures, sharp dialogue, and moments of heartbreaking stillness. It sits in that often-overlooked place between urban and rural, in a landscape too often dismissed as 'in-between' but which holds a wealth of cultural memory and lived experience. James doesn't exoticise this place, nor does he romanticise it. He writes it as he lived it, with grit, nuance, and deep affection.

And yet, this is not just James' personal story. This is a story for a wider Australia—an Australia that still struggles to see beyond the inner city when it comes to defining our national culture. Very few Australian plays centre working-class, non-Anglo families, particularly those in outer suburban or semi-rural communities. And fewer still, do so through the lens of queerness. James is changing that. He is one of a growing number of artists whose work insists that our stages reflect the full spectrum of who we are—culturally, socially, and emotionally.

Karim challenges the way we frame 'Australian stories' by asking why so many exclude the very communities who have helped build modern Australia. James' Lebanese heritage is integral to the world of *Karim*, but it is never used as a mere backdrop. His work refuses tokenism. Instead, he invites the audience into a complex, intergenerational world shaped by migration, faith, family obligation and resilience.

Religion, race, bigotry, and queerness intertwine in *Karim*—not as issues to be explained, but as realities to be lived through. Karim's queerness, for instance, is not a subplot or an add-on. It shapes his experience in quiet, consistent ways—through navigating his father's expectations, through social silences, and through the unspoken compromises he has learnt to make. In these moments, James gives voice to a generation of queer migrants and children of migrants who are too often caught between pride and shame, visibility and invisibility, belonging and exile—of truly being everywhere and nowhere at the same time.

Beth, another central character in the play, embodies the complexity of loving a place and being hurt by it. In one of the play's most poignant lines, she says: 'One thing I've never told ya. I love it here. I love Tahmoor. Love the bush. The air … I've never felt trapped by it. It's when I go home, that … beauty is drained out of me.' Her words cut to the heart of what *Karim* is trying to say: that it's not always the physical landscape that confines us, but the emotional terrain we are forced to navigate within it.

It's important to note that James was told early in his career that there was no audience for his work, that his stories wouldn't sell tickets or connect with mainstream audiences. That belief has been thoroughly, gloriously disproven. James' work has played to sold-out seasons, resonating deeply with audiences who have waited too long to see their realities reflected on stage. His plays are not only artistically accomplished. They are socially necessary.

At Riverside's National Theatre of Parramatta, we are proud to have been part of James' journey from the beginning. His first professional production, *Lady Tabouli*, was a landmark moment, not only for James but for our company and for the national theatrical landscape. We followed this debut with *Queen Fatima* and now *Karim*, each production building upon the last in depth, ambition and artistry. Supporting James' work has been one of the great privileges of my career. He is a writer of extraordinary courage and clarity; someone who writes not to provoke for provocation's sake, but to tell the truth as he knows it.

The response to *Karim* from our local community has been overwhelming. Audiences in Western Sydney have expressed joy, pride and even relief at seeing their lives on stage, not as stereotypes, but as complex, vibrant realities. One audience member told us, 'I never thought I'd see Tahmoor in a play. I never thought I'd hear an accent like mine on stage.' That kind of validation of place, of language, of experience is profound. It's what theatre, at its best, can do.

Karim also speaks to a much larger context. It reflects the precariousness of life for many Australians today, particularly those living without financial or community safety nets. The characters in this play live close to the edge. They scavenge, make do, improvise. Whether it's for money, affection, dignity, or simply peace, the struggle is constant. There is a scene where scavenging through garbage becomes a metaphor for survival and, heartbreakingly, it no longer feels symbolic. The fragility depicted in *Karim* is not fiction; it is a reality that more and more Australians are facing.

In this way, *Karim* connects rural experience to urban marginalisation. What James shows us is that these worlds are not so different. In both, people are searching for connection, for opportunity, for safety. The scavenger in the country and the person collecting cans in the city are reflections of the same systemic failures, the same lack of care. Through his characters, James reminds us that poverty is not a moral failing, but the result of structures that have long ignored or excluded entire communities.

The final moments of *Karim* return us to the bush, the place where it all began. As the lights fade, we are left with a sense of stillness, of unresolved beauty. The land is constant, even as lives shift and shatter. For James, and for many of us, the bush is not just a setting—it is a character. It holds memory, pain, possibility. It is both the place we long to escape and the place we forever carry.

This play is not simply a work of fiction. It is a cultural document, a mirror held up to a nation still learning how to see itself fully. It is the story of a boy who talked to trees and listened to silence, who was told his stories didn't matter, and who proved otherwise.

We are only just beginning to scratch the surface of these stories that lie outside the mainstream, beyond the inner city and its dominant narrative. Thanks to writers like James, and companies like Riverside's National Theatre of Parramatta who champion these writers, those stories are finally being told with the complexity, compassion and clarity they deserve.

INTRODUCTION

As you read or watch *Karim* on stage, I invite you to think not only about the characters, but about the world that shaped them. About the people in your life who live quietly on the edges, whose stories haven't yet been told. And about the power of theatre to make those stories visible.

Let us keep building stages where all of us can be seen.

Joanne Kee
Executive and Creative Producer,
Riverside's National Theatre of Parramatta

Youssef Sabet as Karim and George Kanaan as Abdul in The National Theatre of Parramatta's production of Karim *2024. (Photo: Phil Erbacher)*

Writer's Note

Karim is deeply rooted in my upbringing in a semi-rural environment, and I genuinely believe this experience has shaped who I am today. Growing up in such a community, you hold tightly to your heritage and culture, yet also feel the pressure to adapt and integrate so you're not left on the outside. In this balance, I often felt caught between two worlds—my Lebanese heritage and my Australian identity—never fully belonging to either. In the end, I had to create my own sense of culture, as that was the only way I could make sense of my experience. At the same time, I didn't want to follow the traditional career paths often found in rural NSW; I yearned for freedom. This desire for independence became the driving force behind *Karim*.

For me, *Karim* is a reflection of the struggle between listening to that quiet voice inside, trusting your instincts, and navigating the weight of familial expectations. It's a delicate balance, and it's not easily resolved.

I would like to express my heartfelt gratitude to Joanne Kee for her unwavering support of my work and my mission to bring untold Australian stories to the stage. Her belief in me has been invaluable. I also want to thank the team at the National Theatre of Parramatta for producing *Karim* and for their exceptional support throughout this journey. Lastly, my deepest thanks go to all the artists involved, including my co-director Shane Anthony, who did an outstanding job. These creatives were dedicated to bringing *Karim* to life in the most beautiful way, and I am forever grateful for their commitment.

James Elazzi

Jane Phegan as Kaye and Alex Malone as Beth in The National Theatre of Parramatta's production of KARIM 2024. (Photo: Phil Erbacher)

Youssef Sabet as Karim and George Kanaan as Abdul in The National Theatre of Parramatta's production of KARIM 2024. (Photo: Phil Erbacher)

KARIM was first performed at Riverside's National Theatre of Parramatta, Burramuttagul Country, on July 25, 2024, with the following cast:

KARIM	Youssef Sabet
JOE	Andrew Cutcliffe
KAYE	Jane Phegan
BETH	Alex Malone
ABDUL	George Kanaan

Director, James Elazzi
Director and Dramaturg, Shane Anthony
Set and Costume Designer, James Browne
Lighting Designer, Frankie Clarke
Sound Designer and Composer, Aimée Falzon
Intimacy Director, Trish Speers
Stage Manager, Saz Watson
Production Manager, D. Andrew Potvin

CHARACTERS

KARIM
JOE
BETH
KAYE
ABDUL
JUDGE 1
JUDGE 2

1

KARIM *and* JOE *go through rubbish piles set for the tip.*

KARIM: Moon's bright.
JOE: Yeah.
KARIM: Don't even need a street light.
JOE: Here is a good pile.

They walk to a pile of rubbish placed on the kerb and begin looking through it.

Nothin' here. Let's keep walking.
KARIM: Wait a minute.
JOE: We're wasting time.
KARIM: Some cups there, down the bottom.
JOE: Where?
KARIM: Under all this other stuff, in a box.
Grey patterns and that.
JOE: Any cracks?
KARIM: Can't see any.
JOE: Pull one out.

A moment while KARIM *observes the cups.*

KARIM: They look good, Dad. China-lookin' cups. Looks like there might be a whole set too.
JOE: Help me move this panel.

JOE *analyses the cup.*

JOE: … Karim, it's plastic.
KARIM: I swear they looked like china.
JOE: Look at it. What does it look like to you?
JOE: Forget it. Pick up those plates though.
KARIM: These plates?
JOE: They're from the sixties. Bag them. Don't make too much noise.
KARIM: All of them?
JOE: All of them.
KARIM: This bag won't fit 'em.

JOE: Make it fit. And we've still got the piles on Maclay Street to get through.
KARIM: Now?
JOE: Right now.
KARIM: What about all these plates I'm carryin'?
JOE: What's wrong with you tonight? Mixing shit up and being lazy?
KARIM: How is this lazy?
JOE: Complaining ever since we left the house.
KARIM: … So this is how you wanna spend your birthday?
JOE: Reckon about this lamp?
KARIM: Bag it.
KARIM: Happy birthday.
JOE: Yep.
KARIM: [*singing*] Happy birthday—
JOE: And I said yep.
KARIM: What's yep?
JOE: Yep for my birthday.
KARIM: Well that's good 'cause 'yep' is the only thing I can afford to get ya. Enjoy it.
    … Would've made a small cake or something if we were home.
JOE: —
KARIM: … If you could have anything right now, what would you want for your birthday?
JOE: Being out here is what I want.

   They continue.

2

KARIM *sits with* BETH *on the roof of Tahmoor Train Station.*

KARIM: College get back to ya?
BETH: Nah.
KARIM: Call 'em.
BETH: What for?
KARIM: Find out if you got in.
BETH: Not worryin' 'bout it anymore and neither should you.
KARIM: Why?

BETH: No difference if I call.
KARIM: Least you're findin' out and that.
BETH: Findin' out what?
KARIM: If you had a chance.
BETH: Train's late.
KARIM: No harm in calling and checkin'—
BETH: I'm not callin' 'em.
KARIM: You wanted to do that course so bad.
BETH: Yeah and I changed my mind. Anyway, Mum's gonna get me a job.
KARIM: Where?
BETH: Workin' with Christie at Skippy's Takeaway on the main street.
KARIM: Shit idea, ay.
BETH: Why?
KARIM: They're always fightin' in that shop. Don't get mixed up in that.
BETH: Boom! Train's here.
    Look at 'em all rushin' to their cars.
    So … what's her story?
KARIM: Blue jumper?
BETH: Yeah.
KARIM: Name's … Cathy.
BETH: Job?
KARIM: Advertising. Big office. Job of her dreams and that.
BETH: Yeah … Who walks round smilin' like that?
KARIM: Cathy apparently. What about him?
BETH: Looks like a … Charlie. Three kids. Wife loves to have sex every Wednesday followed by chocolate ice cream.
KARIM: Chocolate ice cream?
BETH: Yeah. It's Charlie's thing y'know.
KARIM: Looks like a Fred to me.
BETH: Nah Charlie. Charlie for sure.
KARIM: Why Charlie?
BETH: His eyebrows. Only Charlies have thick eyebrows. Bet he's got a nice place.
KARIM: Yeah. With a big oven and that.
BETH: Yeah.

KARIM: What time you goin' back home?
BETH: Hangin' round here for a while.
KARIM: Why?
BETH: 'Cause I want to.
KARIM: When's the next train?
BETH: Hour and a bit.
KARIM: You're gonna sit here all that time?
BETH: Why not?
KARIM: Wanna go for a walk?
BETH: Where to?
KARIM: Frank's Deli.
BETH: Nah.
KARIM: Why?
BETH: No money and I got Mum's ciggies before I came here.
KARIM: I'll buy us ice cream. Too hot to be sittin' up here for another hour.
BETH: Who's makin' you stay?
  Look! Another train? It's not supposed to arrive now?
KARIM: It's definitely stoppin'.
BETH: Must've been delayed?
KARIM: Maybe?
BETH: Only a couple of 'em comin' out. Green bag ... Roger. Lives alone. Has a lot of money 'cause he doesn't have kids and that.
KARIM: Why doesn't he have kids?
BETH: Job-focused.
KARIM: Yeah. Job-focused. I reckon Roger's married.
BETH: What does he do for work?
KARIM: Librarian.
BETH: Yeah?
KARIM: Yeah. Definitely works in a library.
BETH: Looks loaded.
KARIM: Exactly. A librarian.
BETH: Imagine everything you can do as a librarian.
KARIM: Yeah ...
BETH: All them books and stuff. Power.
KARIM: Heaps of power.
BETH: Imagine having all that power.

KARIM: Yeah.
BETH: Maybe we could give him somethin' a bit more exciting to do, like workin' at a … fish 'n' chip shop … or … a pet shop.
KARIM: Pet shop?
BETH: Would love to work in a pet shop …
    Oh that one, with the long black hair.
    … Look at her. That weak smile. Wish I looked like her.
KARIM: You're much prettier, hey.
BETH: You're just sayin' that.
KARIM: No I'm not.
BETH: She definitely lives in the nice part of Tahmoor.
BETH: How lucky. Gettin' picked up from the train station.
KARIM: We've done two trains now. C'mon, I'll buy us chocolate Billabongs from Frank's.
BETH: I'm fine.
KARIM: How long you gonna sit up here?
BETH: … I wanna to look like her. That lady with the weak smile.
KARIM: You're beautiful, Beth.
BETH: I don't see beautiful.
    I see my mum.

    KARIM *gets up.* BETH *remains.*

3

JOE *and* KARIM *go through piles of rubbish.*

JOE: The best piles are outside houses on the quiet streets. You know this.
KARIM: I'm tellin' ya there's some good stuff in this pile.
JOE: —
KARIM: It's an old house and old houses have good stuff.

    KARIM *rummages through the pile.*

JOE: *Get up* and walk to Sully Street with me.
KARIM: I'm gonna find somethin'. Least I tried.
JOE: The only thing you found was wasted time.
KARIM: What?
JOE: You heard me. You see anyone else out here doin' shit like this?

JOE: And that's a good thing!
KARIM: It's freezin'! Can't even feel my toes, nose or nuts.
JOE: The good stuff isn't gonna come running to you … Listen, I promise, three more streets and we go home.
KARIM: There is no good stuff!
JOE: We'll find somethin' in Sully Street.
KARIM: I'm goin' home.
JOE: I need you here with me. You gonna pay that electricity bill with your own money then? It's late by a month!
KARIM: —
JOE: You don't think I'm cold too? Tired! Exhausted.

    I *need* you to come with me.

    We'll head home after Sully Street. Find somethin' worth a hundred bucks. You take fifty.
KARIM: … Use my share for the electricity.
JOE: Bills are mine to deal with.
KARIM: —
JOE: … I was … thinkin' … of movin' away from Tahmoor. Maybe somewhere we can afford to buy some land. Grow our own crops.
KARIM: Buy land where?
JOE: Would have to be a little further out. Goulburn maybe?
KARIM: This lamp.

    *The voice of a neighbour—*ABDUL*—is heard from one of the houses.*

ABDUL: [*voiceover*] Oi! The hell you doin!
KARIM: Piss off!
ABDUL: [*voiceover*] Making the place a mess!
KARIM: Ignore him, Dad.
ABDUL: [*voiceover*] Get off the lawn!
KARIM: Let's go.
ABDUL: [*voiceover*] You hear me!
JOE: It's council property!
KARIM: I said let's go.

    KARIM *and* JOE *walk off.*

4

Tahmoor Train Station. KARIM *sits on the roof looking out.* BETH *approaches.*

KARIM: Thought you were babysittin'?
BETH: Bitch got someone else. Rather be here anyway. Train's runnin' late.

Pause.

KARIM: What changed your mind 'bout the college?
BETH: Nothing.
KARIM: C'mon.
BETH: I don't wanna hear …
KARIM: Go on.
BETH: I know I'm gonna hear those words. 'Beth, you didn't get in' … I don't wanna hear it.
KARIM: You don't know that.
BETH: Sort yourself out before you interrogate me.
KARIM: Is that what you call this? Interrogation?
BETH: —

They pause as they look out.

Hey … I know you like dick and that but … let's play around.
KARIM: What?
BETH: Let's … play around. A little stroke and poke.
KARIM: No.
BETH: Why?
KARIM: Because we're mates.
BETH: And?
KARIM: Mates don't … do that.
BETH: Some do.
KARIM: Not us.
BETH: Train guard's not here today. We can go behind the platform there. A bit of a high, that's all.
KARIM: We're not doin' that.
BETH: Why?

KARIM: Once we do it and it's over, we'll feel like shit.
BETH: Then we do it again.
KARIM: That's not how it works.
BETH: But it can be. Close your eyes and think of someone else if you want.
KARIM: What's goin' on with you?
BETH: What's wrong with a natural high?
KARIM: Stop talking like that.
BETH: You have it way too easy. You got your dad and that. Got each other. You've got an idea 'bout what you're gonna do tomorrow.
KARIM: I got home at two a.m. carrying bags of people's rubbish just to make a few dollars to buy food.
    … Did you have a fight with your mum?
BETH: She's not home to have a fight with.
KARIM: That college—
BETH: I'm not goin' to any college. Don't ask me again.
KARIM: Hey.
BETH: —
KARIM: Wanna go down to Mermaids Pool?
BETH: Don't have me swimmers.
KARIM: Minute ago you wanted to have sex?
BETH: That's different.
KARIM: How?
BETH: We don't need to be completely naked.
KARIM: Let's go to the water. Cool us down a bit.
    … You wanna feel beautiful? Mermaids Pool will make you beautiful.
BETH: How?
KARIM: The water is healing. Heard it does something to the skin. Makes you glow and that.
    The bush makes this special mixture that fills the water. The leaves, the rocks, the dirt. The sun melts all of those things into the water … creates this … kinda magic stream.
    Only us locals know about it.
BETH: I don't know about it?
KARIM: Well-kept secret.
BETH: C'mon.

KARIM: Don't believe me?
BETH: Nope.
KARIM: There's only one way of finding out.
BETH: —
KARIM: Well?
BETH: Might dye my hair black like that lady the other day.
KARIM: Let's go.

   Both exit.

5

BETH's *living room.*

Her mother, KAYE, *lies on the couch.* BETH *covers her with a blanket, goes into the kitchen, makes two peanut butter sandwiches, places one near her mother, and begins eating the other as she sits on the couch beside her.*

6

KARIM *and* JOE *arrive back home holding bags of rubbish.*

KARIM: Dad, the door isn't opening.

   An envelope is wedged between the door and the trim.

JOE: There. Open it.
KARIM: They're evicting us?!
JOE: Try the key again.
KARIM: Did you pay the rent?
JOE: Give me the key.
KARIM: Did you pay the rent?!
JOE: … Things. Things were pilin' up … spoke to the agent a while back, thought we had an agreement. Break down the door with me!
KARIM: And then what?
JOE: Kick it down with me!
KARIM: They'll call the cops and we'll have to pay for it!
JOE: It's midnight! It's bloody midnight! [*Whispering*] It's midnight.
KARIM: What do we do?

JOE: Let me think.
KARIM: You knew this was gonna happen.
JOE: Had no idea.
KARIM: Bullshit.
JOE: Karim—
KARIM: Why didn't you tell me?
JOE: Tell you what?
KARIM: That you couldn't pay the rent.
JOE: I *could* pay it.
KARIM: Yeah!?
JOE: I had the money. I just needed …
KARIM: —
JOE: I needed a little bit of time.
KARIM: You can't even admit it.
JOE: How's this going to help? Us arguing.
KARIM: Because you can't even admit you stuffed up!

> *Pause.*

If I had known, I would've given you my savings.
JOE: Your savings aren't enough.
KARIM: I would've spoken to them. I would've done something! Instead we are out here, with nowhere to go.
JOE: I'm sorry.
KARIM: —
JOE: Karim. I'm sorry.

> *The neighbour,* ABDUL, *fifty-eight years old, walks outside, watches on.*

[*To* ABDUL] Sorry, mate. Nothing to see here.
ABDUL: —
JOE: The assholes changed the locks while we were out.
  [*To* KARIM] Wait here.
KARIM: Where you going?
JOE: We need somewhere to stay tonight.
KARIM: Let me go with you.
JOE: Keep the stuff we've found tonight with you. I'll be back.

> JOE *goes.* KARIM *stands still.*

7

BETH *and* KAYE*'s home.*

KAYE: Baby.
BETH: You're awake?
KAYE: Awake and makin' ya brekky!
BETH: Up so early?
KAYE: Easy to wake up early when the morning sun calls your name.
BETH: Look at you, smilin' and all.
KAYE: Disability payment with a bonus came into my account this mornin'! Bought us some eggs, that yoghurt you like. Some chips ... frozen pizzas ... we're set, baby girl. Toast?
BETH: You havin' some toast too?
KAYE: Course I am.
BETH: I'll make it.
KAYE: Nope. I got ya. House needs a good clean too.
We'll clean it together. Watch a movie later?
Casablanca?
BETH: Sounds good.
KAYE: I'll get us some popcorn. And those chocolate bullets you like chewing with the popcorn.
Did you call Skippy's?
BETH: I will today.
KAYE: Yeah call 'em. Christie's gonna hire ya. Spoke to her last week. Said she'll take ya on. Told her you're good with your hands and that.
All you'd be doin' is chopping red tomatoes and slicing lettuce, makin' them burgers for the truck drivers. Sellin' ice cream and lollies ... it's a really cushy job, baby girl.
BETH: Sounds good, Mum.
KAYE: You'll call her today. Mate, I'm feelin' good!
BETH: —
KAYE: Bill mowed our lawn yesterday arvo. Always does his and goes right to our fence line but stops. Never comes across to our lawn.
But then yesterday, baby, yesterday he mowed our front yard. I'm feelin' the love. Bill mowed our lawn and I'm feelin' loved!

KAYE *hands* BETH *some toast. She looks out the window.*

BETH: Where's your toast?
KAYE: Will have some in a sec. Look at that morning sun bursting in here, Beth.
BETH: Yeah.
KAYE: C'mon, eat up. I'm gonna start cleanin' up the bathroom in a sec.

KAYE *looks out the window once more.*

BETH: What's outside?
KAYE: Nothin'.
BETH: Waiting for someone?
KAYE: Nah, baby, checkin' that mornin' glow, that's all.
BETH: Here, have one of my toasts.
KAYE: No no, eat your toast. Made it the way you like and everything.

BETH *looks out of the window.*

BETH: Mum.
KAYE: Bathroom then kitchen.
BETH: Mum. What's he doing here?
KAYE: Who?
BETH: Him. In that car.
KAYE: He's not comin' inside the house.
BETH: I thought you were stayin' home today?
KAYE: I am.
BETH: Then tell him to piss off.
KAYE: Baby—
BETH: I don't want you goin' out there.
KAYE: It's my business alright? You and I, we got plans today, don't you worry 'bout that.
BETH: This is why you're up early.
KAYE: It's not like before. I promise.
BETH: Thought you wanted to watch a movie?
KAYE: We are.
BETH: *Mum—*
KAYE: Don't start. It's too early in the morning for your shit. It's my house. I do what I want. I'm gonna be home all day and you got me all day and night. No-one's goin' stone cold.

Look I'm feelin' good. Strong. Don't you waste the feeling of that sun bursting in here.
BETH: —
KAYE: I made ya brekky didn't I?
BETH: —
KAYE: Didn't I?
BETH: … Yeah.
KAYE: Finish and then call Christie for that job.
… Us two. Watching *Casablanca*, hey.
Who's me baby girl?

    KAYE *exits.* BETH *stands in silence.*

8

7.30 a.m. JOE *and* KARIM *sit at* ABDUL*'s kitchen table having a light breakfast.*

JOE: I'm goin' to the cucumber farm to find work.
I'll try and get ya work there too.

    ABDUL *enters.*

I promise you, Abdul, we'll be outta your hair in no time. Honestly appreciate you taking us in like this.
ABDUL: I've been in worse situations.
JOE: It's humiliating.
Karim, watch those crumbs.
ABDUL: Not at all. So they changed the lock whilst you were gone?
JOE: Bloody assholes.
ABDUL: Were you behind in the rent?
JOE: … Couple of weeks.
Maybe a tad longer. There was a mutual understanding with the agent.
ABDUL: There's no understanding when money isn't paid.
JOE: How long have you lived in Tahmoor?
ABDUL: 1981 moved to Picton. Then Tahmoor in '86.
JOE: Any family around here?
ABDUL: Some relatives live in Sydney.
JOE: So here by yourself?

ABDUL: By myself.
JOE: Must get a little lonely around here?
ABDUL: Cucumber picking must be hard work?
JOE: … Lebanese cucumbers and restoring things people throw out is all I've ever known. Karim, yallah help clean up.
ABDUL: I'll wash up my own plates.
JOE: Karim will do it.
ABDUL: It's fine.
JOE: Here. Money for what we've eaten.
ABDUL: No.
JOE: If we're stayin' here, we pay our way.
ABDUL: Keep your money.
JOE: Please, mate. Take it. Don't argue with me. Otherwise we can't stay here.
ABDUL: Joe, we all face times like these.
JOE: I appreciate this. [*To* KARIM] Yallah. I'm goin'.

>JOE *notices two paintings.*

Not bad … Nude bodies and all.
ABDUL: It's about the flow, movement and shade of the body …
JOE: Yeah. Shade and that, yes. Can I ask … how much is one of these bad boys?
ABDUL: About ten thousand for that one. Maybe fifteen for that other one.

>JOE *laughs.*

JOE: C'mon … mate. Abdul. I'm so sorry.
ABDUL: For?
JOE: You've been scammed.
ABDUL: How did they scam me?
JOE: Painting like a kid and making you pay thousands for it.
ABDUL: That's the set price.
JOE: For who?
ABDUL: Me. The buyer.
JOE: You willingly paid ten thousand?
ABDUL: Because I love the pieces.
JOE: Why?
ABDUL: Its beauty. Encapsulated. In my home.

JOE: Mate, I'll buy some paint and paint you something ... 'encapsulated'.
ABDUL: If you were Norman Lindsay.
JOE: I'll absolutely be whoever you want me to be. [*To* KARIM] I'm gonna find you the best bloody paintbrush and you're going to be painting day and night. And I'm calling you Normal bloody Lindsay from now on.
KARIM: I can't paint.
JOE: Yep. Course you can't. I gotta go.

    JOE *exits*.

ABDUL: You'll be working in a cucumber farm soon too?
KARIM: Yeah.
ABDUL: How long have you been doing that?
KARIM: In between slow periods of rubbish tip pickin'.
ABDUL: How old are you?
KARIM: Just turned twenty-three last month.
ABDUL: Good money in rubbish tip picking?
KARIM: Depends on what we find. Music records are like gold and vintage furniture but it's hard to carry it back without a car. Never found paintings like yours though.
ABDUL: No, I wouldn't think so.
KARIM: Once I found a twenty-four-karat ring. Ate like kings that night ... anyway, Saad the farmer pays us ninety bucks a day in cash. So it's alright.
ABDUL: Good skill to have: vegetable picking.
KARIM: Yeah.
ABDUL: Once you learn a skill and it makes you some money, you can get stuck, especially out here, in Tahmoor. Of course, there's nothing wrong with cucumber picking.
KARIM: We've been picking cucumbers in our family for generations. Dad prefers restoring furniture though.
ABDUL: What about you?
KARIM: Me?
ABDUL: Enjoy what you are doing?
KARIM: Guess so. Was tryin' to get into uni and that. Biology.
ABDUL: You like Biology?
KARIM: Don't even know what it is. But it sounded good.

ABDUL: Why would you even think about doing it then?
KARIM: Something to do other than farming. Another way out of Tahmoor.
ABDUL: Out of Tahmoor?
KARIM: [*smirking*] We don't have this. A place where we look out to the gum trees and the arvo sun. Surrounded by artworks that cost more money than I've ever seen. All I see is sweat, rubbish and greenhouses filled with spiky veggie leaves.

But Dad always tells me, 'every time you fail, you fall back on things you know'.
ABDUL: And that's rubbish tip picking and Lebanese cucumbers?
KARIM: I end up failing most things.
ABDUL: Do you read?
KARIM: Read what?
ABDUL: Books. You do know what a book looks like?
KARIM: I'm not stupid.

> ABDUL *picks up a book.*

… *Gate of the Sun* by Elias Khoury.
ABDUL: It's a good one.
KARIM: [*looking over*] … Strange-lookin' guitar?
ABDUL: An oud. A Lebanese musical instrument. You should know it.
KARIM: No idea. You play it?
ABDUL: I haven't for years.
KARIM: It's beautiful.

Shame you're letting it rot here.
ABDUL: I played the oud for the Lebanese Symphony Orchestra for seventeen years before the war.
KARIM: Dad's never mentioned a war?
ABDUL: Because he was born here. But your grandparents would know. In 1981 I escaped the Lebanese civil war with nothing but this oud.
KARIM: So you went to all the trouble of takin' this with ya from Lebanon with bombs goin' off but you don't play it?
ABDUL: Nostalgia is a wasteful thing we become obsessed with.
KARIM: … I'm gonna head to the shop.
ABDUL: Here. Take your dad's twenty.

> KARIM *takes the twenty.*

KARIM: Dad will wanna see what I've bought. Otherwise he won't stay here. And I … wouldn't mind stayin' here a little bit longer.

9

Midnight. KARIM *goes to the cupboard where the oud is placed. Takes it out and looks at it.*
He glides his hand up and down the oud, wiping some dust with it. He picks it up and analyses it. He places it down.

10

Night. BETH *walks into her living room with two bags of popcorn.* KAYE *sits on the couch, high, and finding it all too humorous.*

BETH: Got us popcorn.
KAYE: What flavour?
BETH: You okay?
KAYE: What flavour?
BETH: Just salted.
KAYE: Popcorn's gotta have a flavour! Flavour is the way of life and life's not worth livin' without flavour!
BETH: You're high.
KAYE: Me? No-one's high here. I'm just waitin' for that popcorn to pop into my mouth. And you're the annoying one that's standin' there askin' questions!
BETH: Here, take your packet.
KAYE: How many packets did you get?
BETH: Twelve pack.
KAYE: I'm loved.
BETH: Yeah.
KAYE: I'm definitely loved. A twelve pack. In case I finish this one and want another, hey.
BETH: Yeah, you're loved.
KAYE: Taught you well.
BETH: What?
KAYE: What? Pop!
BETH: What do you want to watch?

KAYE: Anythin' you want. Anythin' this world has to offer. Pop. We're all just popcorn popping away!
BETH: *Casablanca*?
KAYE: —
BETH: Mum?
KAYE: What?
BETH: *Casablanca*?
KAYE: Any movie, I don't care.

> KAYE *scratches her skin.*

Did ya?
BETH: What?
KAYE: Close it?
BETH: Close?
KAYE: The fly screen? Did you close it?
BETH: Yeah.
KAYE: You always leave it open.
BETH: I've never left it open.
KAYE: I seen ya leave it open. Those mosquitos always biting' the hell outta me.
BETH: There's no mosquitos.
KAYE: You do it on purpose.
BETH: —
KAYE: I know you do.
BETH: Okay.
KAYE: Did you close the fly screen when you came in?
BETH: Eat your popcorn.
KAYE: Go check it.
BETH: I'm lookin' at the fly screen. The door is shut.
KAYE: Get up and check it.
BETH: I can see it.
KAYE: Get up!

> BETH *gets up and checks the fly screen.* KAYE *bursts out in laughter.*

BETH: The kitchen is filthy.
KAYE: Yeah and?
BETH: Thought you were gonna clean it.

KAYE: *Casablanca* is waiting for us.
BETH: I'll get ya some water.
KAYE: Put on the movie or I'm going to bed. Pop!
　　　Check the fly screen.
BETH: —
KAYE: Don't just stand there and stare at me like a idiot. Check the fly screen! I'm gettin' bitten.
BETH: *The fly screen is shut.*
KAYE: Now I'm ready to be taken away with the film. Put the film on.
BETH: Not in the mood anymore.
KAYE: Yes you are.
BETH: —
KAYE: I said yes you are.
BETH: No.
KAYE: I stayed home to watch a movie, and that's what we're gonna do.
KAYE: That look.
　　　That look you're givin' me. You look like him. That ugly prick. Stop looking at me. Pierce right through me you do. Can't stand it. I can't stand him. Why'd you bring him here!
BETH: Stop—
KAYE: Why'd you bring him here?

　　　BETH *exits.*

You look exactly like him. You keep bringin' him back here. Don't look at me, don't do that!
　　　Close the fly screen.

11

BETH *and* KARIM *stand at Tahmoor platform.* BETH *has a backpack on.*

KARIM: Got your message?
BETH: Took you long enough.
KARIM: What's the rush?
BETH: I'm leavin'.
KARIM: What?
BETH: Leavin' this shithole. Catchin' the three-twenty-one train.
KARIM: Where you goin'?

BETH: Sydney. Gonna live with my Aunty. It's only an hour and a half away.
KARIM: She know you're comin'?
BETH: She will once I'm there.
KARIM: What you gonna do in the city?
BETH: Anythin'.
KARIM: What about your mum?
BETH: Once the meth wears off, she might call.
KARIM: Where'd you get the money for the ticket?
BETH: I didn't.
KARIM: And when the train guards check?
BETH: I'll manage. Come with me.
KARIM: I can't.
BETH: Come with me. I know you wanna leave this place.
KARIM: Dad's here.
BETH: Here? Where's here? Pickin' rubbish and cucumbers ... In Sydney, it'll be us two, finding our way and that?
KARIM: Dad's workin' hard to sort everythin' out.
BETH: Suit yourself. Gonna forget Tahmoor ever existed. I wanna be in the right place at the right time. Never gonna happen here.
KARIM: I'm gonna miss you. Better call me.
BETH: Maybe.
KARIM: Maybe?
BETH: You'll miss me for the first couple of days, but then after that you'll get on with things.
KARIM: Hate when you say shit like that.
BETH: It's how it is. How things work.
KARIM: I'll visit you if I ever come to the city.
BETH: If that's what you want?
KARIM: Let me know when you arrive.
BETH: Don't have credit.
KARIM: Here. I've only got fifty.
BETH: Don't want money.
KARIM: Can I get a hug?
BETH: No. That might be the reason I don't go. Be good habibi. Train's gonna come and take me away.

BETH *exits.* KARIM *watches her walk down the platform.*

KARIM *watches* JOE *get ready to work on the cucumber farm.*

JOE: Yallah. Get ready. We're leavin' in a bit. Go wash your face, have somethin' to eat. Don't be loud.
KARIM: Got a call from uni yesterday.
JOE: And?
KARIM: They want me to come in.
JOE: For what?
KARIM: About the course.
JOE: What course?
KARIM: Biology.
JOE: Not that bullshit again.
KARIM: I wanna try it out.
JOE: You're going to miss out on a day's work on the farm.
KARIM: Biology might good.
JOE: The hell you know about biology?
KARIM: It's science and … that.
JOE: Uni is not gonna pay you. Tomorrow you're comin' with me.
KARIM: Tomorrow.
JOE: I told Saad he could rely on you at the farm. Don't make me out to be a liar.
KARIM: He can.
JOE: Karim, you're not the university type.
KARIM: I wanna at least try.
JOE: Don't eat any of Abdul's food.

    JOE *exits.* ABDUL *walks into the kitchen.*

KARIM: Did we wake you?
ABDUL: No. I usually get up early and water my plants. Coffee?
KARIM: No.
ABDUL: Thought you were going with your father to the farm?
KARIM: Told him I'm busy.
ABDUL: Have you been reading that book?
KARIM: Not yet.
ABDUL: I see the oud grew feet and walked out of the cupboard?

KARIM: Can you teach me?
ABDUL: —
KARIM: How to play it.
ABDUL: Play the oud?
KARIM: Yeah.
ABDUL: Am I missing something?
KARIM: I wanna give it a shot.
ABDUL: … I'll make a coffee.
KARIM: Great.
ABDUL: I'll make you one.
KARIM: I'm fine. I'll get changed and we can begin?

> KARIM *goes to his bedroom, making sure* ABDUL *is in sight. He takes off his shirt facing* ABDUL. *They share a glance.* ABDUL *then looks away and begins making a Lebanese roll.* KARIM *comes back.*

Tell me more about the Lebanese Symphony Orchestra.
ABDUL: Before the war, Lebanon was filled with art. Music. Growing up, I'd play the oud on a busy street. People would give me coins, and I'd buy whatever I wanted. A man named Isayeh noticed me and before I knew it, I was playing the oud in the orchestra. I played festivals, concerts, the biggest singers: Sabah, Whadi El Safi, Samira Toufic … I earned enough money to buy my parents a home, enough to live a good life. The oud did that, gave me the best. Then the war hit. Raped the country. Turned it into rubble. Religion, money for ammunition and possession of land poisoned Lebanon.
  … So this curiosity about the oud?
KARIM: What sound does it make?
ABDUL: Ever heard of Fairuz?
KARIM: No.
ABDUL: What kind of Lebanese people are you?
KARIM: Lebanese by face, nothing else.
ABDUL: Sit down. Place your hands here, on the side of the oud.
  When they bombed my village, I grabbed this oud and ran. People, holding onto their little babies, jewellery, photos … crying, screaming … and there I was, desperately holding onto this, people yelling to leave it behind. It's worthless …

I thought this oud would provide for my future here. But Australia and the oud in the eighties was a terrible match.

But it became a reminder: when I'd play it, instead of hearing the strings, I'd hear screaming.

KARIM: And now?

ABDUL: If someone else plays it, it's fine.

Here. Hold it. Open your arms to it.

ABDUL shifts over.

KARIM: No need to move away.

Am I holdin' it right?

ABDUL: Relax your grip, your shoulders. Let it balance lightly. Like this. Learning an instrument takes years. The oud is the same, but with dedication, it can be very easy to learn, creating the most exquisite sound.

Get a feel of what you can create with your fingers.

KARIM: Show me how you want me to hold it.

Curious tension between them. ABDUL *takes the oud and begins playing it.*

ABDUL: Forget the western instruments you know. What they taught you at school. There are musical instruments that create immersive sounds that remove you from here and take you on a journey. No guitar, piano, drums … it's the oud, tablah, daf, buzuq, qanun that make you fly.

KARIM: I have no idea what you are saying but I like it.

ABDUL: You have an eyelash.

ABDUL removes the eyelash.

KARIM: … I love the sound.

ABDUL: That's because you feel a sense of connection to the oud. A musical instrument that comes from the same place your ancestors come from.

ABDUL continues playing the oud, which bleeds into the next scene.

13

KAYE *is on the phone.*

KAYE: Please, mate. I promise, come round next Wednesday and I have some coin for ya.
 I'm not goin' anywhere. You know where I live. Mate, please. I need this ... Alright. I'm inside waiting.

14

KARIM *meets* BETH *in Tahmoor Train Station.*

BETH: Got as far as Ingleburn. Mum called, started cryin' when she heard I was on a train. I hate when she cries. Guilt is gonna ruin my life.
KARIM: Don't be too hard on yourself.
BETH: How do I leave Mum?
KARIM: Don't know.
BETH: ... Ever felt freedom?
KARIM: Maybe?
BETH: I felt it for a moment, ay.
KARIM: What did it feel like?
BETH: Air. Like breathin' in air for the first time. Even on the train, I inhaled that air in. Deep into my lungs. Down into my guts. Made it fill me up.
 I smiled as the train was flyin' me away. Air and trains: combine those two and you've got ... freedom. But here I am. Back here.
KARIM: [*trying to hide his smile*] Yeah.
BETH: Look at you.
KARIM: What?
BETH: What's makin' you smile?
KARIM: Nothing.
BETH: C'mon dickhead. Tell me.
KARIM: ... I'm into someone.
BETH: Who?
KARIM: He's a little older.

BETH: You can't keep rooting Mr Robinson. His wife and kids will find out sooner or later and blame you.
KARIM: It's someone else.
BETH: Yeah?
KARIM: And it feels really good, hey.
　　　Kinda like this excitement inside me, running through my belly down between my legs, balls, and then my feet. Makin' my steps lighter. Yeah … lighter.
BETH: Who is it?
KARIM: Abdul. And he's gonna help me learn the oud.
BETH: That old Muslim guy with them red roses out the front?
KARIM: Yeah.
BETH: I *knew* he liked dick. And what's an oud?
KARIM: A musical instrument. Looks like a bigger version of a guitar. I'm gonna learn it. When I heard him play it, it felt like I was in this other world I didn't know existed.
BETH: Maybe I should learn to play it too?
KARIM: Won't suit ya.
BETH: Piss off!
KARIM: It won't.
BETH: What's good for you, is good for me.
　　　… Look at that smile.
KARIM: I can't help it. It feels so …
BETH: Good.
KARIM: Yeah. Real good, Beth.
BETH: … I wanna feel that excitement inside my body too, into my guts, down between my legs; just like you.
KARIM: I'm sure you will, hey.
BETH: … Yeah.
KARIM: I'll play the oud for ya sometime too.
BETH: … Playing the oud. Learning, unlearning, what does it matter? We all come back to where we started. We always come back.
KARIM: —
BETH: I can tell ya right now, there is no-one here that will make me feel the way you're feeling right now.
KARIM: —
BETH: I'm gonna get stuck here, aren't I?

KARIM: We gotta make a plan.
BETH: … Play the oud for me sometime.
    They both sit still.

15

BETH *walks into her house carrying some groceries.* KAYE *sits on the couch waiting for her.*

KAYE: … Look at you!
BETH: Bought ya some Twisties. The big packet and that.
    I'll put 'em in a bowl?
KAYE: You got the nerve to speak?
BETH: Glad you're up.
KAYE: Been waitin'.
BETH: I got some other stuff from the shop.
KAYE: I been waitin' all day for you.
BETH: Hungry?
KAYE: Did you hear me?
BETH: I'll make ya a sandwich if you want?
KAYE: Where were you goin'?
BETH: Doesn't matter.
KAYE: It matters.
BETH: I'm here now.
KAYE: On that train. Where were you goin'?
BETH: —
KAYE: Open your mouth and tell me.
BETH: I'll make ya a cream cheese.
KAYE: You wanna be away from me?
BETH: —
KAYE: Away from your own mother?
BETH: —
KAYE: I asked you a question?
BETH: I'm gonna make some.
KAYE: Where were you goin'?
BETH: —
KAYE: This place ain't good enough for you?

BETH: Mum—
KAYE: I'm not good enough? Say it. Your mumma not good enough? She causing you problems? Hmm? After everythin' I've done for you?
BETH: You?
KAYE: —
BETH: What have you done?
KAYE: —
BETH: What have you done for me?
KAYE: Remember who you're talkin' to yeah.
BETH: Who am I talkin' too?
KAYE: Me.
BETH: Who are you?
KAYE: [*face to face*] Your. *Mother.*
BETH: My mother? *Where is she?* Cryin' on the phone when you knew I was leavin'.

    I had somewhere to go.
KAYE: You got nowhere to go. *Nothing.* No-one. I'm all you got and when I'm not around, you got nothing.
BETH: —
KAYE: You can't leave me. I'll never let you.
BETH: [*whispering*] I hate you.
KAYE: Say it again.
BETH: I. Hate you.

    KAYE *slaps* BETH.

    They pause.

KAYE: I'm … I'm sorry, baby. Beth. I'm sorry! I'm sorry. I love you. I love you so much, baby. I love you. I'm here. I'm right here. Don't you mention that word hate, you hear. I never wanna hear it. That word shakes me. Kills me.

16A

KARIM *and* ABDUL *stand in* ABDUL*'s house.*

KARIM: Dad only had about seven boxes to go when I left and then coffee with the guys on the farm. I'll get the oud.
ABDUL: Go back to the farm and help your dad.
KARIM: Since when did you care?
ABDUL: It's the right thing to do.
KARIM: Being here is the right thing for me.
ABDUL: Then go back and tell him I'm teaching you how to play the oud. It's been two weeks.
KARIM: If Dad knows I'm rushing back here to play the oud, he'll move right out. I'd have to go with him.
ABDUL: You don't have to go anywhere with him.
KARIM: Let's begin the oud lesson.
ABDUL: [*smiling*] Look at you.
KARIM: —
ABDUL: So serious?
KARIM: I'm very serious.
ABDUL: That's a good thing.
KARIM: … You're wearing cologne.
ABDUL: Am I?
KARIM: Wearing cologne for me.
ABDUL: Don't be so sure of yourself.
KARIM: [*smirking*] You smell good.
ABDUL: —
KARIM: If I had cologne, I'd wear it too. For you. But right now you're going to have to deal with the smell of sweat and pesticides.

    ABDUL *laughs.*

ABDUL: I needed that laugh.
KARIM: Your eyes light up when you laugh.
ABDUL: Do you like that?
KARIM: Very much.
ABDUL: Then you better keep me laughing.
    … The oud.

KARIM: [*picking up the oud*] Abdul, teach me how to be great on this.
ABDUL: And then what? You'll end up back at the farm?
KARIM: Depends how good my teacher is.
ABDUL: … How does it make you feel, holding it?
KARIM: Like I been holding it for years.
ABDUL: Cradle it.
KARIM: Like this?
ABDUL: Keep your neck up to avoid straining your neck later on.

> ABDUL *is close to* KARIM. KARIM *plays the oud.*

Remember, as you continue practising, the oud consists of five fundamental components: the body, the soundboard, the neck, the peg box and the strings. The body is made first in the construction process.
… Do you like that?

KARIM: Love it.
ABDUL: How much?

> KARIM *kisses* ABDUL. KARIM *stops.*

KARIM: Can I do that again?

> *They kiss once more.*

16B

Montage.

BETH *covers* KAYE *with a blanket.* KARIM *plays the oud.* JOE *packs cucumbers. He gets up, holds his back in pain.*

17

KAYE *sits on the couch holding popcorn packets.* BETH *enters.*

BETH: You cleaned the place?
KAYE: And made some sandwiches. Cheese and tomatoes. They look good, hey.
BETH: —
KAYE: Did you see them?
BETH: —
KAYE: Them sandwiches I made for us.

BETH: Yeah.
KAYE: I put a little bit of salt and pepper on 'em. The way you like.
BETH: Alright.
KAYE: Cheese, tomato and lettuce. Had no idea lettuce lasted so long in the fridge. You have to rip the outer leaves off. Even if they look rotten outside, inside they're still good, baby.
BETH: Yeah?
KAYE: Yeah. Two weeks and that lettuce still has that crunch.
 Here. All yours. Made with all my love.
BETH: Sandwiches and love.
KAYE: Yep … I lost my temper before. I'm sorry.
BETH: —
KAYE: I'm sorry, baby. Forgive me?
BETH: Yeah. I'm fine.
KAYE: That's my girl, hmm.
 You know why you forgive me?
BETH: Why?
KAYE: 'Cause I added pepper and salt, the way you like.
 No-one knows you like your mum.
BETH: —
KAYE: Guess what? No more meeting anyone. Don't need it. Cold turkey. I can do it. I am doing it.
 I swear, this time it's different. I'm done. I don't need anyone's help in being done either. I can do it alone. Doing it for you. For us.
BETH: … For us.
KAYE: Come here. Sit next to me.
BETH: —
KAYE: Please.
BETH: —
KAYE: Don't you be angry at me.
BETH: You do this so well.
KAYE: Beth—
BETH: All I do is go up and down. That's all I end up doin'. Up and down. I'm so tired, Mum.
KAYE: Come and sit next to me, baby.
 Please … Please.
 My baby girl. What would I do without you? Hmmm. My angel.

My mum, your nan, told me once 'bout this magpie. It would come onto her verandah out the back. This massive bird, all silvery and black. She'd tell this bird everythin'. 'Bout me leavin' her for weeks and not callin' her. I was a bad daughter, ay. Made me mum worry all the time ... so that magpie turned into Nan's only company. It was something Nan looked forward to every day. Something constant.

She never had that before. Something ... reliable. Everyone she would meet would always end up leaving her. Even I left her. Left me own mum.

I ran away with him, your father. He always said I'd get no-one better than him. Made me believe when the world looked at me, all they'd see is this ugly, odd-lookin' woman. He made me feel I was lucky to have him. Lucky he looked at me the way he did. And I believed him. And I stayed. I stayed with him year after year. Nan, she told me to leave him ... but I was stubborn.

He showed me suffering he did. Beat me down to the bone. The week I finally told your father to piss off, your nan died. I had no idea. For weeks, I was flying high, smoking in that white cloud, feet not touching the ground. All the while your nan was deep in the ground. They told me she was dyin' but I never listened.

Too late for me now. I'm not worthy of her forgiveness. But here, baby, *here* ... there is beauty in you stickin' around. For me, you are my forgiveness. Don't go on and leave me.

I got no magpie.

Only you.

18

KARIM *takes his shirt off.* ABDUL *cleans* KARIM*'s body with a cloth.*

KARIM: Look. More blisters on my fingers from playin' the oud.
ABDUL: The skin will become impenetrable.
KARIM: No-one has ever taken time with me ... like you are doing right now. I'm no-one.
ABDUL: To me, you stand out like nothing else.
  Say it.
KARIM: I'm a farmer. Pickin' cucumbers because pickin' rubbish wasn't making enough money.

You make me feel as though I'm at the front of the line. And this oud … first time I've ever been good at somethin'. I wanna be you, grabbin' onto his future but not forgettin' the past. Makin' a new version of myself. Making a new life …

Learning how to play this oud, I'm a step closer. Making music. I'm making music?

Yeah. Me.

ABDUL: That smile.

KARIM: Yeah?

ABDUL: It's … cheeky. Ever had a boyfriend?

KARIM: Yeah. Guy my age … he was a dickhead. I like 'em older. They know what they want. Stable. That turns me on. Stability and that.

ABDUL: Very mature of you?

KARIM: When I was a kid, I saw what Dad's face looked like when he'd hold Mum. Kinda like … bliss. When she died, his face never looked like that again.

… I want a man to make me feel like that.

ABDUL: I lied to you before. The truth. The war broke out and I escaped here. In this new country, I wanted to live openly as a gay man. I met Ben shortly afterwards. I found the courage to tell my family, most of them cut me out besides my mother. I didn't want the headache so moved out here. To the bush.

KARIM: Tell me more about Ben.

ABDUL: Twenty-three years. Died ten years ago. He loved the sound of the oud. The sound is a picture of a man I loved. Now, when you play it, you ease that pain.

KARIM: I'm glad. What … what about sex?

ABDUL: What about it?

KARIM: You don't feel it?

ABDUL: I head to the city.

KARIM: You don't need to head to the city anymore.

ABDUL: Your father wouldn't be happy about this.

KARIM: Yeah. He doesn't care who I sleep with, as long as I live and work with him.

My heart beats like crazy when I'm around you.

ABDUL: Karim … I'm much older.

KARIM: Yeah and I love that. I love your white hair. The creases on your skin. The way your body feels, I'm lit in every possible way. I want you and everythin' you bring to me.

ABDUL: Show me by playing Raqsat al-Gamal (Farid Al-Atrash).

> KARIM *picks up the oud and plays a short mediocre version of any tune.*

KARIM: What am I missing?

ABDUL: Just before you are about to play, people will wait with curiosity. Then you become the master, taking the audience on a journey with you …

> KARIM *plays with more fluidity and passion, then stops.*

KARIM: I wanna stay here. With you. Dad's plannin' to move out. But I wanna stay here.

ABDUL: I … don't know, Karim.

KARIM: Don't know what?

ABDUL: If that's a good idea.

KARIM: I'll pay my way. I will be workin' and everythin'. This way, I will have much more time to learn the oud and … and we'll be here together.

ABDUL: —

KARIM: Abdul?

ABDUL: I don't want you to misunderstand me.

KARIM: Misunderstand what?

ABDUL: I don't want to be the cause of trouble between you and your father.

KARIM: What trouble?

ABDUL: He relies on you.

KARIM: Tell me you don't want me here.

ABDUL: I feel like I'm going to be stuck in the middle.

KARIM: This is what I want. Do you?

ABDUL: —

KARIM: Do you want this?

ABDUL: The way I feel right now … it's been so long. But your father won't understand this, us.

KARIM: I want this so much.

> KARIM *dips the cloth into the water.* ABDUL *removes his shirt and* KARIM *begins to clean* ABDUL*'s chest.*

ABDUL: Slower.

19

ABDUL *exits and is replaced by* JOE *who cleans up on the farm.*

JOE: Slowly. Slower. That's it. That's it … Fill the oud with your blood. The oud is an extension of your body. Keep going, Karim. Keep going until you are satisfied.

KARIM: [*confused*] What?

JOE: Are you listening to me?

> JOE *picks up two boxes of cucumbers and begins sorting them.* KARIM *places the oud down, and now is on the farm working with* JOE.

Seconds go here.

KARIM: That's where I've been putting 'em?

JOE: You've been putting the seconds with the firsts.

KARIM: No I haven't—

JOE: I'm constantly pickin' out your seconds because you're rushing. Every single day. You're rushing.

Makin' my job harder. What's so important?

KARIM: Nothing.

JOE: You must take your time sorting them.

What's the rush anyway?

KARIM: No rush.

JOE: You mess up, it doubles up my work.

KARIM: —

JOE: Nowhere more important than here. The job that pays you.

KARIM: Is this cucumber a second?

JOE: Yes.

KARIM: But there's nothin' wrong with it?

JOE: It curves to the side.

KARIM: It's still good.

JOE: It's classed as a second and you know this?

KARIM: What a waste.

JOE: I don't make the rules round here. No-one wants to buy curved cucumbers.

KARIM: I don't mind 'em.

JOE: Course you don't.

    KARIM *laughs.*

KARIM: Ey.

JOE: Curved cucumbers, straight cucumbers—

KARIM: Okay Dad. Okay.

    They pack. KARIM *is hurried, once more.*

JOE: … There you go again. Rushing!

KARIM: Alright, Dad. Alright.

JOE: No more rushing.

    They continue in silence for a moment.

Makin' money doin' something you're familiar with. It's a blessing, habibi. Grow some crops. It's a beautiful thing. Workin' on the land. Farming is in our blood, Karim.

    You ever thought about buyin' something …

KARIM: Buyin' what?

JOE: Land. Me, I … I can't do it. I don't have time to save all that money … but you, habibi, you're young. You can become a success out here.

KARIM: Pickin' cucumbers?

JOE: Buyin' a farm. You'd never regret it. We always come back to what we know. The seeds here, the crops, allow 'em to make you money. One day we could live like kings.

    Your great-grandfather, he was a proud man. A farmer who knew how to work this land. But your grandfather … he messed it up, gambled, sold the land. But with us, we can begin again. You are the new generation.

KARIM: You've never spoken about Lebanon.

JOE: Lebanon? Why would I speak about Lebanon?

KARIM: That's where we come from?

JOE: I was born here. So was your grandfather.

KARIM: But that's our heritage.

JOE: All I know is what's in front of me.

KARIM: I wanna know more.
JOE: More about what?
KARIM: Our history.
JOE: I've never been to Lebanon.
KARIM: What about the war?
JOE: We've been in Australia way before the war, Karim.
KARIM: Never been curious?
JOE: I'm too busy trying to make ends meet and that kills curiosity.
KARIM: Do you know the oud?
JOE: ... That guitar?
KARIM: Similar but makes a completely different sound.
JOE: How do you know?
KARIM: I just know, hey.
JOE: ... You just know?
KARIM: Saw it on telly.
JOE: On the telly? ... Keep goin' with those cucumbers. Also, two more days and we move out of Abdul's.
KARIM: What?
JOE: We've been there for almost three months.
KARIM: Where we goin'?
JOE: We'll stay here. On the farm.
KARIM: Where on this farm?
JOE: Couple of farmers were livin' in that shed over there. They're movin' out ... so I asked about it. Even scored us a good deal with the rent.
KARIM: The grey farm shed?
JOE: It's got everythin' we need.
    We can't stay at Abdul's forever.
KARIM: There's nothin' round here besides greenhouses?
JOE: Exactly. There's work. They've converted the shed inside. Little kitchen and all that.
KARIM: You been inside?
JOE: Yeah.
KARIM: How am I gonna get around?
JOE: Get around where?
KARIM: The shops, whatever ...
JOE: Bargo Train Station is down the road.

KARIM: That's an hour-and-a-half walk.
JOE: Why do you need to catch the train anyway?
KARIM: It's an option.
JOE: Option for what? Where do you need to be other than here? Trust me. This is what we need to do.
KARIM: —
JOE: Nothin' beats having your own place.

    JOE *exits.* ABDUL *enters.*

20

ABDUL *and* KARIM *continue with the oud.*

ABDUL: Stop rushing.
KARIM: I'm not.
ABDUL: You are.
KARIM: I can't get it. I always stuff up this string.
ABDUL: Keep going—
KARIM: This top string, I can't get it.
ABDUL: Calm down.

    KARIM *begins again. And then stops.*

KARIM: Shit!
ABDUL: Slower. Go slower.
KARIM: I can't get it!
ABDUL: You are rushing. You need to give it time.
KARIM: I feel like I'm at the start again. Always coming back to the start.
ABDUL: You've improved so much.
KARIM: But nowhere near where I thought I would be!
ABDUL: Just take a moment, breathe in and go again.
KARIM: —
ABDUL: Karim, learning an instrument and being fluid with it takes years.

    KARIM *goes to wear his farm clothes.*

  Where are you going?
KARIM: Where I belong.
ABDUL: What?

KARIM: It's too hard. I'm done.
ABDUL: Pick up the oud and start again.
KARIM: What's the point?
ABDUL: *Come back here and pick up the oud.*
KARIM: I'm going to the farm.
ABDUL: Come back here.
KARIM: Been at it for weeks! For what!
ABDUL: … I knew it! I knew you were going to do this.
KARIM: I have spent hours! Hours running back and forth every day and practising this bullshit! Thinking it would get me somewhere.
ABDUL: Where do you think it would get you?!
KARIM: Far from here! Far from where I'm standing!
ABDUL: A lack of patience gets nothing.
KARIM: Enough of your bullshit talk. I've wasted so much time here.
ABDUL: You know what, alright, Karim. Go to back your life, where you belong.
KARIM: What did you say?
ABDUL: Your poor life. What you deserve.
KARIM: You're a prick.
ABDUL: Took you this long to realise?
KARIM: A *prick*.
ABDUL: Hurry up. The greenhouses are waiting for you.
KARIM: I feel sorry for you.
ABDUL: My life is absolutely complete.
KARIM: You have nothing here without me.
ABDUL: You're right. I am lonely. So I used you. But I was always going to throw you back to your father because you're useless.

> KARIM *picks up the oud and is ready to slam it on the ground.*

No!
KARIM: I could get this piece of wood and smash it into a million pieces!—
ABDUL: Please don't—
KARIM: This rotting piece of wood!—
ABDUL: Please! Don't. Please. Put it down …

> KARIM *relents.* ABDUL *grabs the oud and cradles it.*
>
> *Extended pause.*

KARIM: I … I'm … I'm sorry … I'm sorry.
 You know … you know I would, I *could* never break it.
 I need it as much as you.
ABDUL: —
KARIM: Pass it to me.
ABDUL: What?
KARIM: Pass it to me.

 KARIM *begins playing it.*

ABDUL: … Slow … Steady. Every string accounted for. You will get there.
KARIM: Hey.
ABDUL: —
KARIM: I'm stayin' here.

 KARIM *continues.*

21

KARIM *continues playing the oud.*

As KARIM *plays the oud,* JOE *packs cucumbers into boxes, then stops for a moment, holds his back from the pain and then begins again. Box after box.*

BETH *watches* KAYE *sleeping on the couch and covers her with a blanket, then walks over and sits on top of Tahmoor Train Station.*

22

JOE *walks in.* ABDUL *stands in the kitchen with* KARIM.

JOE: Some of your clothes are still on the clothesline outside.
KARIM: Yeah I know.
JOE: So go and take 'em off? I've packed all our jumpers in that blue bag.
KARIM: Dad—
JOE: They have some pots and shit in the shed already. We can use what they've left behind. We'll go shopping though, get what we need, pepper, flour, the staples—
KARIM: I don't wanna move into that shed on the farm.

JOE: What?
KARIM: I wanna stay here.
JOE: Where's here?
KARIM: Here. With Abdul.
JOE: What do you mean, with Abdul? … You two? … What's goin' on here, Karim?
KARIM: I've been learning the oud and everythin'.
JOE: The oud?!
KARIM: That musical instrument I was telling you about the other day.

> KARIM *picks up the oud.*

This.
JOE: Pack your shit up. I don't have time for this.
KARIM: Dad—
JOE: Pack your clothes up or we leave them here.
KARIM: Abdul, tell Dad about the oud.
ABDUL: —
KARIM: Tell him how I play.
ABDUL: He …
JOE: He what!
… Are you … are you sleeping with my son?
KARIM: Dad—
JOE: Are you?
ABDUL: It's not like that.

> JOE *grabs a bag and throws it at* KARIM.

JOE: Pack your shit now.
KARIM: I'm stayin' here!
JOE: Can't you see what's goin' on here! That old pervert is usin' you!
KARIM: I want this. It's me!
JOE: You don't know what you want!
KARIM: This is what I want!
JOE: What are you gonna do when he's had enough of you?
KARIM: It's not like that.
JOE: When he is sick of you, you'll come runnin' back to me like a failure.
ABDUL: He isn't a failure.
JOE: What?
ABDUL: He isn't a failure. The way Karim plays the oud, he is … brilliant. So much potential.

>   JOE *grabs* ABDUL *by the neck.*

JOE: How long you been sleeping with him?—
KARIM: Let him go—
JOE: How long!
KARIM: Get off him!

>   ABDUL *pushes* JOE *to the ground and kicks him in the stomach.*

Stop!

>   KARIM *pushes* ABDUL *away from* JOE.

Don't you touch him!
ABDUL: Get out of my house. You and your father. I knew this would happen!
KARIM: What?
ABDUL: Take your shit and leave.

>   KARIM *picks up his bag and goes.* JOE *slowly gets up holding his stomach. He walks over to the oud and rips out two strings from it.*

>   ABDUL *doesn't move.* JOE *picks up his bag and exits.*

23

KARIM *waits for* BETH *on the roof of Tahmoor Train Station.*

BETH: One with the grey jacket … The way she walks. That's power, ay.
KARIM: —
BETH: And that one … what's her name?
KARIM: —
BETH: Karim?
KARIM: What?
BETH: What's her name?
KARIM: … Kate.
BETH: Kate? Nah, she looks like a wog. Maybe a Greek. Let's call her Fifi. Yeah. Fifi. Greek power bitch. And her handbag's expensive. Makes good food and that. Greek food. Bet it's delicious, ay. Like olives and feta.

Yeah Olives, feta and tomatoes. Greeks: they live a long time apparently. She's wearing a leather buckle too. Easy four hundred. Easy.

Over there. Ken. A tradie. But doesn't need his van on Tuesdays. Attention to detail. See what I'm doin'.

KARIM: I'm tired of being here.
BETH: Then look out and tell me who all those people are.
KARIM: —
BETH: How's that oud stuff going?
KARIM: It's not.
BETH: Why?
KARIM: —
BETH: Wanna go to Mermaids Pool?
KARIM: No.
BETH: I always went for you.
KARIM: —
BETH: Even when I didn't want too. I always went there to be with you.
KARIM: —
BETH: Let the water heal you.
KARIM: —
BETH: I'm listening?
KARIM: I wanna sit here alone.
BETH: You either come with me to Mermaids Pool, or we sit here all day and night.
KARIM: I don't want you here.
BETH: What?
KARIM: I don't want you here with me.
BETH: You don't get a choice.
KARIM: —
BETH: I'm here.
KARIM: I don't want you here.
BETH: And I said, *you don't get a choice* ... Come here.
KARIM: —
BETH: ... Let me hold you.
KARIM: No.
BETH: Bury your anger right here.

Pause.

Come. Here.

After a moment, KARIM *allows* BETH *to hold him.*

Don't ever cut me out.

I'll act like I don't care, but it hurts.

KARIM: —

BETH: And it hurts just that little bit more because it's you.

KARIM: … I never once felt like comin' up here when I played the oud. I was getting there, getting to a feelin' of being proud.

BETH: Keep playin' it. Don't stop.

KARIM: … Thanks, hey.

BETH: For what?

KARIM: This.

BETH: What am I doing?

KARIM: Holding me.

BETH: Don't ever thank someone for holding you.

KARIM: … Tell me something. Get my mind off things.

BETH: … I've always been a talker, hey. Chat so much, to everyone and everything. It's how I made sense of the world. Talkin'. In Year Six, Mrs Greeson made me sit right at the front of the class for a whole year, thinkin' that would quieten me down. It didn't. I just ended up talking to her. I wanted the world to see me, y'know … I've never felt that with you. Felt the need to yap on. Could sit here for hours and not say a word 'cause with you, *you* make me feel heard. Holding you right now is the closest thing that's ever felt like home.

They stay embraced.

24

ABDUL *walks onto the farm where* JOE *is putting wet clothes on the clothesline.*

JOE: What are you doing here?

ABDUL: I've come to see Karim.

JOE: Piss off.

ABDUL: Is he here?

JOE: I said. Piss off.

ABDUL: I need to tell him one thing and I'm gone.

JOE: No.
ABDUL: He is a grown man, he can decide himself.
JOE: You got no idea who you're dealing with.
ABDUL: I didn't come here to speak to you.
KARIM: What are you doin' here?
ABDUL: Take this. It's an audition for a scholarship with a musical company looking for an oud player in Sydney. In three weeks' time. I know the guy that runs it, so I must take you.
KARIM: —
ABDUL: You've got what it takes. This scholarship only opens up once every two years.
KARIM: —
ABDUL: I'll drive you.
JOE: God, why don't you just piss off out of our lives—
ABDUL: It's a rare opportunity, Karim—
JOE: Like a cockroach—
ABDUL: Karim—
KARIM: No—
ABDUL: All the work we did?
JOE: You heard him. Get into your car and go.
ABDUL: Are you sure?
KARIM: —
ABDUL: Are you?
KARIM: Yeah.
JOE: You heard him.
KARIM: This is where I need to be. It's clear as day. I'm building my name here.
ABDUL: Building?
JOE: I told you piss off—
ABDUL: Building what? What the hell are you building!?
JOE: Thought you were a decent bloke, taking us in and all.
ABDUL: —
JOE: Get outta here before I do something I will regret.

    ABDUL *exits*.

I'm sorry.
KARIM: For what?

JOE: Trusting a stranger.

Look out, over the farm, as far as the eye can see. This open land. Our paradise. Take it all in habibi. Take this land and tear the ground up and make something of your life, hmm. Maybe one day you meet a good man. A younger man … fall in love with him. Have a good life. Maybe a farmer. Same as you. Livin' out here, but keepin' your old man close to you.

I've been called a failure, but they can't see what I see. I'm not gonna go and buy an expensive house livin' in the city with the rest of them. Praying to a God that doesn't exist. Here, on this land, this is God. Your mum felt the same y'know, before she died.

All I need is you, hard work and a few dollars, and I'm a happy man. Follow my lead, Karim.

I know you may think there might be something a little better out there. But I would tell ya. I'm showin' you what I have seen and learnt. I would never lead ya astray. Love you, boy.

KARIM: Love you too.

JOE exits. KARIM stays still.

25

KAYE *sits on the couch, high and confused.* BETH *enters.*

BETH: … Mum? What are you doing?

KAYE: I got big plans.

BETH: I'll make you a tea.

KAYE: Big, big plans. I've got them. Plans.

BETH: Mum—

KAYE: You proud of me?

BETH: What plans?

KAYE: I'm gonna get a big job. You're all gonna be proud of me.

BETH: Mum?

KAYE: Every single one of you will be tellin' me how good I am.

BETH: —

KAYE: I'm not a failure. Nope. Not me.

BETH: Please, Mum.

KAYE: Don't you be standing there lookin' upset. I'm gonna fix us. That's my job. Fixing. My job, the suit I'm gonna wear. You can rely on me.

BETH: Mum, stop.
KAYE: Stop worryin'.
BETH: God. I am sick of this.

    KAYE *laughs.*

KAYE: Baby, I gotta job?! Me!
BETH: —
KAYE: I'll come home on Fridays with that money, take you out to a nice restaurant.
BETH: —
KAYE: I've made big, big mistakes, but look, I'm good. I'm gonna be the mum you need. My mum, well, she was a big problem. But me, nope. I'm doing well.
BETH: What have you taken?
KAYE: Don't you cut me out. I know you will eventually. And when you do, it will be like someone cutting out me guts.
BETH: We can't keep doing this.
KAYE: I need to rest now. I have a big day ahead of me. Don't you keep me up, you hear. I'll be making money, and all of you will be begging to have some.

    BETH *packs a bag quickly.*

Why you got your bag?

    BETH *continues.*

Snake. You're a little *snake.*
BETH: I don't wanna hate you, Mum, but if I stop hatin' you, I'll begin to hate myself. And I can't do that. I won't. I'm lookin' at you and I'm startin' to see my reflection.
KAYE: You ain't got hate for me, girl.
BETH: What do I do? I don't know what to do?

    BETH *exits.*

KAYE: I got a job. A big job. Me a business woman. My mum, she wouldn't believe it, hey, always goin' on about me being a failure and that.

    KAYE *laughs.*

I'll show her. I'll show her what her daughter can do.

Pause.

… Beth? Iron that new dress suit I got. I have to look me best, y'know.

BETH *looks around and nods.*

I'm gonna make it all better.

I'm a mother. A mother of a snake. [*Disgusted*] Look at you.

After a moment, KAYE *lies down on the couch and passes out.*

26

Tahmoor Train Station platform. Silence as BETH *stands alone.*

KARIM: Packed a bag and everythin'?

BETH: Everything I've got fits in it.

KARIM: You're not comin' back this time, ay.

BETH: I need you to do somethin' for me. Visit my mum once a week. Make sure she's alright and that. Promise me.

KARIM: I promise.

BETH: If there is no food, buy it. I left a hundred and ten bucks under the purple rock out the front. I'm trustin' you okay?

KARIM: I will. I'll check up on her …

Silence.

BETH: Something has changed in you.

KARIM: Harvesting and that.

BETH: No point lyin'.

KARIM: —

BETH: *Come with me.*

KARIM: —

BETH: Karim.

KARIM: Can't leave Dad.

BETH: I can't leave Mum. But I am.

KARIM: I'll be alright, hey. What's the first thing you're gonna do?

BETH: Look at you changin' the subject …

I'm gonna tell aunty, tell 'em all what's goin' on with Mum, y'know, get 'em all involved. There's only so much I can do alone.

Even if they don't want a bar of it, they'll know what's goin' on here.

BETH: … So you're stayin' here huh?

KARIM: Never had a choice.

BETH: I'm giving you one now.

KARIM: I can't come with you.

BETH: Alright. I'm nervous.

KARIM: If things turn to shit, blame me. If you get to Sydney and things stuff up. Blame me.

Sit on that train and let it take you away.

BETH: You need to take your own advice.

KARIM: —

BETH: No you're not. This place can drown you.

KARIM: Don't you come back here.

BETH: One thing I've never told ya. I love it here. I love Tahmoor. Love the bush. The air … I've never felt trapped by it. It's when I go home, that … beauty is drained out of me. So I go back to that creek behind our place and restart. But now even the bush has no power. Bought that packet of black hair dye, remember? Stared at it for hours. It's just stupid hair dye. No, it isn't just hair dye. All I seem to wanna do is lose myself.

I'm doin' the right thing, hey, Karim?

KARIM: Nothing else you can do.

BETH: It's already hurting.

KARIM: That's love. But you can love your mum from afar. Alright?

BETH: Alright.

They embrace.

Train's here … I love you, Karim.

KARIM: If you really love me, you get on that train and don't come back.

BETH: Alright.

KARIM: Past Ingleburn.

BETH: Past Ingleburn. All the way.

They continue holding each other. BETH *exits.*

KARIM: I love you too, Beth.

KARIM *stands still.*

KAYE *walks up to the farm shed.* JOE *hangs clothes on the line.*

KAYE: Mate.
JOE: Ms McDowell?
KAYE: Been a while.
JOE: It has.
KAYE: How's it all goin' here?
JOE: Good. I'm assumin' you're here to talk to Karim?
KAYE: Yes.
JOE: Right. What's this about?
KAYE: It's ah … personal, mate.
JOE: Personal?
KAYE: Yeah. Between me and Karim.
KAYE: Look if you've got somethin' to say … say it.
JOE: You clean?
KAYE: —
JOE: Don't want you bringing any trouble here.
KAYE: Come and search me. Here. Check my bag.

>   JOE *takes her bag.*

You're actually gonna do it?

>   JOE *searches it.*

Found nothing, hey?
JOE: —
KAYE: Can I have me bag back? Cheers. Listen, mate, I didn't come here to cause trouble. I came to talk to your boy. Nothin' else.
JOE: … Karim. You've ah, got a … visitor.

>   KARIM *enters.*

KARIM: Mrs McDowell?
KAYE: Hi, mate … can we ah, have a little chat?

>   JOE *shakes his head and exits.*

All those greenhouses. Hard work, ay?
KARIM: Sure is.

KAYE: Always thought I should give it a go. Sweat it out a little.

KARIM: I'm sure the boss wouldn't mind an extra pair of hands. We start at five a.m. in the morning.

KAYE: I think some doctor actually told me I might be allergic to cucumbers.

KARIM: Allergic?

KAYE: Yeah. You can't do anything if you're allergic. Y'know.

KARIM: No five a.m. wake-ups then?

KAYE: Nah …

KARIM: So how'd you get here?

KAYE: Walked.

KARIM: All the way from Tahmoor?

KAYE: Not that far. Especially when you've got a head full of thoughts. You're ah, close to Beth.

KARIM: She's my best mate.

KAYE: She's always goin' on about Karim this, Karim that.
Glad she has a mate like you.

KARIM: Love her like my sister.

KAYE: She left most of her clothes behind. She hasn't called me. Assume she's gone to Sydney?

KARIM: Dunno?

KAYE: Please.

KARIM: I don't know where she's gone.

KAYE: I know what you're thinkin', I do. Stuff up anythin' good that comes into my life.
Beth … I've done nothin' in this life worth bein' proud of, but I'm proud she's my baby. Doesn't matter how much I mess up, I can still call her that. Call her my kid. My girl.
… I ah, I called her number. She won't answer.

KARIM: —

KAYE: Did she ever mention me?

KARIM: Always.

KAYE: What would she say? You be honest with me.

KARIM: That she loves you like nothin' else.

KAYE: She said that? Let me hear that again.

KARIM: … She loves you. Like nothin' else.

KAYE: Like nothin' else.

KARIM: Don't go lookin' for her. If you love her and that.
KAYE: Was callin' her name last night. I was so thirsty. Usually she'd come with a glass of water. I laid there, callin' her name. She's not there anymore. Tonight I'll call her name again. Don't care what anyone thinks. I'm gonna keep callin' her name.

    Am I makin' you feel uncomfortable?
KARIM: No.
KAYE: You're a good boy. Listening to me and that.

    … You happy here?
KARIM: All I need is this land, hard work and a few dollars, and I'm happy.

    Sometimes my mind wanders, thinking there might be somethin' better out there. But I trust Dad.
KAYE: When your mum was alive, we'd sit under that massive oak tree down the main road. She'd tell me her plans about leavin' Tahmoor. She wanted choices. But, mate, when you get sick, there are no choices.
KARIM: Why did she wanna leave?
KAYE: She thought you wouldn't have a future here. Guess your mum didn't know that you'd love farming like you do.
KARIM: … Ever been to Mermaids Pool?
KAYE: Years ago.
KARIM: Beth loves goin' there. We'd spend hours in the water. The healing water.
KAYE: Maybe I'll go past now, on the way home.

    Karim. What do I do without her?
KARIM: Call her name. At night. In the day. If that brings you comfort. Keep callin' her name.

    KAYE *exits.*

KARIM *knocks on* ABDUL*'s door. After a moment,* ABDUL *opens.*

ABDUL: What are you doing here?

KARIM: How long will it take to drive to that audition in Sydney?

ABDUL: What?

KARIM: Mum wanted to get out of Tahmoor and Dad never told me. So. I'm gettin' out. Right now. With you.

ABDUL: —

KARIM: Please. Let's go.

ABDUL: That's not how things work.

KARIM: I know we didn't book an audition but if we are physically there, they'll let us in—

ABDUL: They won't see you. It's too late.

KARIM: I'll get the oud.

ABDUL: I'm not taking you.

KARIM: Why?

ABDUL: I don't need this. To be involved in trouble. This bullshit that I have found myself in.

KARIM: Abdul—

ABDUL: I want peace.

KARIM: There will be no trouble. Please. Let's go.

ABDUL: Your dad will come here lookin' for you, and you harvest today. He needs you.

KARIM: Drive me to Sydney.

ABDUL: Catch the train, it's not that far.

KARIM: I read the letter you gave me. I need to book an appointment and I will have a better chance if I go in early.

ABDUL: Get a lift.

KARIM: Who am I going to ask?

ABDUL: —

KARIM: Drive me to Sydney—

ABDUL: You hurt me! You hurt me!

  I let you into my home. Into my heart. I opened my life to you! I came to your front door and begged you to come with me, and now? Now when it suits you, you want me to drive you?

KARIM: I … I'm sorry.

ABDUL: You being sorry only means you can't get what you want from me now. Go home.

KARIM: Where's home?! I stand there out the back of the farm and I beg those bloody old gumtrees to speak back to me. Beg 'em to answer my question: why does the blood rushing through my veins feel like it's unattached to my heart? … It's just blood rushin' around, feeding what needs to be fed.

I live on this farm and the land is open. Unbarred. But all I feel is claustrophobic. All of it is this tiny little dark room with four walls.

My dad waits for me in that little shed. He has fried eggs, cut up a tomato, broken bread, and he sits there waiting for me. He won't take a bite to eat until I'm there, eating with him. How can I ignore that?

I sleep in a tiny shed with a man who has tried his best to build me a home. And then you. You come, and bring that oud and it opens up this empty land that I'm living on, and that dense bush that is closed off from me begins to burn. The gum trees, the shrubs, the birds … it's all set alight. Flames. But that oud doesn't burn. It's waiting for me. Giving me a glimpse of who I could be. What I could be. And that lust is enough to keep me goin'. The land begins to whisper answers to my questions. Tellin' me that Dad will be alright. Won't suffer, because he will eventually understand what I need to do.

But now, now you take the oud away.

And so there I am. Back in that small shed. Frying eggs, cutting a tomato and breakin' bread.

Waiting for Dad to join me. Just like he did for me.

And when he is right there, we begin to eat. And I look out the window, and once more, the land begins to suffocate me. I don't say a word. Don't move a muscle. And … I finally stop wanting. Because it's too late. I'll begin to wear my father's face. Begin to move like him. Think like him. Smell like him. I become him. Every day repeating over and over.

Abdul, you don't owe me anything, but I hoped you would.

Please, Abdul. Take me.

ABDUL: Your father tore out the oud strings.

KARIM: Do you have duct tape?

KARIM *follows a lady into another room where two* JUDGES *sit behind a long table, each with notepads. An empty chair is placed in the centre.*

JUDGE 1: The first applicant is running late. So very fortunate for you.
KARIM: Yes. Very.
JUDGE 2: The oud is one of my most favourite instruments.

    KARIM *awkwardly smiles.*

Position yourself however you find most comfortable.

    JUDGE 1 *reads awkwardly.*

JUDGE 1: 'We're looking to diversify our collection of musical artists and instruments. Open up, for the first time, artists that rarely have an opportunity. Giving visibility.'
JUDGE 2: Diversity is key. And key is diversity.
JUDGE 1: Where is the case for the oud?
KARIM: Not sure, hey.
JUDGE 2: You don't know?
KARIM: Guess the case was left behind when Abdul was running for his life in the Lebanese Civil War and trying not to get shot in the head.
JUDGE 2: Hmm.
JUDGE 1: Alright then.
    You reside in Tahmoor?
KARIM: Yes.
JUDGE 2: How was the drive?
KARIM: Got into the car with Abdul and he drove me, parked the car, and here I am.
JUDGE 2: How long was the travel here?
KARIM: 'Bout two hours. Traffic and that.
JUDGE 1: Do you work?
KARIM: Yep. Rubbish tip picking and picking Lebanese cucumbers.
JUDGE 1: … Karim, we assume you've read the guidelines on how this audition will pan out?
KARIM: I've read … ah, everything, yes.
JUDGE 1: Great.

KARIM: Actually, can you … It's really early, can you just go over the main points?

JUDGE 2: You may play any piece on the oud you wish. A showcase of your ability. A piece that connects with you, if you will.

JUDGE 1: I'm sure you understand. This isn't about initial skill or clarity of the instrument, we will teach you that. It's moreso about your connection with the instrument.

JUDGE 2: Do you understand, Karim?

    KARIM *nods.*

When you're ready.

    KARIM *picks up the oud, noticing the duct tape around its end. As he attempts to play 'Mar Mar Zamani' [Fairuz], the sound is poor, and when he tries again, the duct tape comes undone, causing him to stop.*

The instrument is broken?

KARIM: I need a moment.

    KARIM *tries to fix the duct tape.*

Actually, do you have a spare oud round here?

JUDGE 2: No.

JUDGE 1: Actually, we may have a spare—

JUDGE 2: We absolutely cannot allow that.

KARIM: Why?

JUDGE 2: That would essentially mean we are giving you an unfair advantage.

JUDGE 1: I'm sure we could find a slot?

JUDGE 2: Our codes of conduct are here to allow for a fair and equitable assessment of applicants.

    Surely you knew a broken instrument would not suffice?

KARIM: —

    I've come all this way.

JUDGE 2: So have many others. Fairness is imperative. Preparation is paramount Mr Hadoum.

    KARIM *tries to play the oud again. The strings become detached once more.*

You can stop now.

KARIM *doesn't stop.*

Time is up.

KARIM *stops.*

JUDGE 1: Karim, the scholarship is open every two years.
KARIM: Two years?
JUDGE 2: We thank you for your time.
KARIM: I'll tighten the duct tape round here, give me a sec—
JUDGE 2: Thank you, Karim.
KARIM: … How will I know?
JUDGE 2: Know what?
KARIM: If I got in?
JUDGE 1: Unfortunately no instrument was played today, so no feedback is required.
KARIM: I'll wait all day, I don't care.
JUDGE 2: Thank you for your time.
JUDGE 1: Two years may seem a long time, but you must continue to play.

Eventually KARIM *exits.*

30

ABDUL *and* KARIM *walk to the cucumber shed.*

ABDUL: Here, keep the oud.
KARIM: What for?
ABDUL: I fixed the strings for you. It's good to go. Take it. Keep practising.
KARIM: Don't need it. But thanks for drivin' me.
ABDUL: It's not over.
KARIM: I went all that way and I wasn't even close. Nowhere near. I don't belong in a room where the walls reflect my face back at me.

JOE *enters.*

JOE: Where were you?
KARIM: I need to get changed.
JOE: What were you doing with him?
KARIM: Doesn't matter.

JOE: It matters if you went with him.
KARIM: I went to Abdul. *I* knocked on his door. *I* asked him to take me to audition.
JOE: You left me to do the morning harvest alone!
KARIM: Did you hear anything I just said?
JOE: You'll never learn, because whatever you went for, you failed.
KARIM: You're right, I failed.
JOE: Wake the hell up, Karim!

> *As* JOE *walks away,* KARIM *picks up the broken oud and starts playing, capturing* JOE*'s attention. Suddenly, the present world dissolves, transporting us into* KARIM*'s vivid imagination—bold and electric, where the sounds of the bush blend with the oud.*
>
> *The stage bursts with life, lights enhancing the surreal atmosphere, while abstract, warped sounds accompany his passionate freestyle. The music flows through* KARIM*, but after a few minutes, he abruptly stops, breathing deeply as he returns to the present in Tahmoor, still clutching the oud.*

THE END

www.ingramcontent.com/pod-product-compliance
Lightning Source LLC
Chambersburg PA
CBHW050023090426
42734CB00021B/3400